LISTENING

to *God*

in the

GARDEN

Spiritual Growth Related to Gardening

SARAH LAWRENCE

Quantum Discovery
A LITERARY AGENCY

Library of Congress Control Number: 2024927028

ISBN
979-8-89641-022-5 (Paperback)
979-8-89641-023-2 (eBook)
979-8-89641-021-8 (Hardcover)

Table of Contents

Acknowledgments

I would like to express a special thanks to my oldest son David Long for his generous help in preparing this book. I knew I could count on you to be totally honest and tell me what needed to be improved or changed. Thanks.

I also want to thank my youngest son Cody Long for being so patient with me when I was on the computer. He was so understanding and just as excited as I was to write this book. Thanks for seeing how important this was to mom.

I want to express my gratitude to my pastor, Chris Hamilton, for always keeping me in line by preaching the truth, even when it hurt. (like picking okra) I thank God for my pastor, his family, and my church family. I would not be where I am today if not for them.

This book is also written in memory of my late husband, Steve Long. He spent countless hours in the garden with me. Steve went home to be with the Lord on June 21,2007.

And last but not least, I want to say a special thanks to my parents, Mary Tudor and the late Paul Tudor. They taught me great family values, morals, and the love of Christ. Thank you.

Introduction

I was inspired by God to write this book. Every year that I planted a garden I learned something new. Lessons in the garden were often about gardening, but they were also about life.

It has been truly amazing at what all God has shown me throughout the years while working in my garden. After a few years of trial and error, I realized God was speaking to me through the garden.

We begin with preparing the soil and go all the way to harvesting the crop. Every aspect of the garden is related to our Christian life and how God wants us to live. Read and see how God spoke to me through gardening.

I hope you enjoy this book as much as I have enjoyed the experience in it myself. God speaks to us all in many ways. We simply must learn to listen to his voice. May God bless you as you learn to listen to God in everything you do.

Throughout this book, many scriptures are listed. I have taken these scriptures from the King James Version of the Bible. Please take time to read the verses. They are very important. Also, I recommend you look up the scriptures in your own bible. Study the Word and read any footnotes your bible may have.

I have also written a few questions you can use as personal study or in group discussions.

My First Garden

I remember as a teenager, I could hardly wait to turn eighteen so I could move out on my own. You know how it is, no parents to tell you what to do, come and go as you please, and stay up late at night. It was an eye opener when the only house I could afford to rent was not well insulated and I nearly froze that winter. By mid-January I moved out. My brother and I together rented a bigger, nicer house. I was so excited when I saw a garden spot in the yard. I couldn't wait to grow my own garden.

I was so happy to get the chance to make a vegetable garden. My papaw Tudor always grew a large garden every year. My dad had always put out a very small garden each year, so I knew a little about gardening, or so I thought.

My dad tilled the ground for me and my older brother helped me plant the seeds and hoe the garden. It was not a bad garden for an eighteen-year-old. As a matter of fact, it was three times bigger than the garden my dad usually made, and nearly everything was very plentiful. I was proud.

I will never forget how excited I was when I picked my first mess of squash. (My brother always went to the garden and ate the cucumbers before anyone else got a chance to even pick one.) I proudly gave away lots of things from my garden, including some of the biggest squash I'd ever seen.

After about the third or fourth big bag of squash I so happily gave to a neighbor, he asked me if I knew that squash was only good to eat when they were small. (He measured with his hands about four to five inches.) Although embarrassing, it was my first lesson learned in the garden.

Needless to say, that was my first lesson in the garden. I was only eighteen and it was my first garden. I can't say that I heard from God that year, but it was the beginning of many lessons I would learn in the garden.

It was many years later and several trials and errors in the garden that I did finally realize, God was speaking. So, I begin listening to God in the garden. Just like my first garden, we often think we are doing things right. We do not always have wisdom as our elders often do. God will put people in our lives to help us grow. Sometimes we receive nuggets from people that will grow so much more in life. Those nuggets we often refer to as seeds. As my neighbor told me how those extra-large squash was no good; it was not a happy moment, but I learned a big lesson. The same in our Christion life, sometimes those nuggets do not make us happy, but if we listen, God will bless us.

Philippians 4:13
I can do all things through Christ which strengthens me.

As I read and studied God's word, I had read Matthew 13:1-23; and Mark 4:1-20; and Luke 8:4-15. The parable of sowing seeds is a powerful study in itself. Although my book does not exactly bring out this particular story, it does relate in some ways. However, as I sowed seeds, hoed weeds, and picked crops; I begin to hear the voice of God speaking to my soul. I listened carefully to what He was showing me.

Throughout this book we will discuss different aspects of gardening and how every step can relate to our spiritual life. Each year as I did the work in my garden, God showed me how each step of gardening did relate to our life. I may have only learned one thing new each year, but as the years went by, I finally looked back and even when I wasn't listening, He was teaching.

Take time now to get your bible out and read these verses.

Matthew 13:1-23
Mark 4:1-20
Luke 8:4-15

I accepted Jesus Christ as my savior when I was only nine years old. I was baptized at the age of thirteen. I began teaching Sunday School at the age of twenty-five. I am now in my fifties and I'm still not perfect. I have learned not to judge others, but to teach with love. *God sent not his Son into the world to condemn the world; but the world through Him might be saved. (John 3:17)* My garden has never been perfect. I have taken no classes to learn how to garden. All my knowledge comes from trial and error.

It was always amazing to me every single year as I planted a tiny seed into the dirt, how, after some water, fertilizer, and sun, it would grow into a great plant that produced more fruit. All that from one tiny seed. I go through that same awe every year. It never gets old.

A lot of times in grammar school, teachers will allow their students to plant a seed in a cup. They water it, put it in the sun and in a couple of weeks they have a tiny plant. Eventually they must transplant it into a larger pot or put it in the ground. It grows and the child has the giddish feeling of awe. They are so excited at the growth of the seed they had planted. We can have that same satisfaction when we plant seeds of Christ in others and see them grow.

Like in my first garden, we will not know everything. We will mess up and get things wrong. God is a loving God. He will forgive us, and we will learn as we go through life. We will experience trials and tribulations through life. Sins will come and go into our life. We must fill our hearts with God's word to help grow our faith. By allowing God to speak to our heart, we can help others to grow as well.

As I had begun my journey in gardening, God had begun a work inside of me. It was as if I was the seed inside the ground being watered and fertilized to begin sprouting. As the sprouts begin to grow, the roots grow deeper and deeper as the plant grows up and out. As time went by, I was nourished and fed throughout life until I begin to produce fruit. My roots became grounded in Christ as I grew, and I begin feeding others.

As you read through this book, we will use different stages of gardening and how it relates to our spiritual lives. Please use your Bible as you read this book and take notes to help remind you where you are and where you need to grow.

Write about a time you heard God speak to you.

_____

_____

_____

_____

_____

Preparing The Soil

One year as I was talking about getting the ground prepared, God spoke to me and showed me I am the ground. I am the garden. Get the ground ready. Prepare the soil. I was not sure what that meant at first. My husband and I discussed turning the ground and putting a load of mushroom dirt on it and tilling it in.

So how do you relate this spiritually? How do I prepare the soil? By preparing the soul! The things I did to prepare the soil for sowing seeds included turning the ground, picking out the rocks, removing glass pieces, and adding fertilizer (mushroom dirt) and tilling it in.

Turning the ground relates to turning our life. When you accept Jesus Christ as your personal savior, you turn your life away from a life of sin to a life of Christ. We are to turn away from sin. Accepting Christ is just the first step into Christian living.

Acts 26:18 says, "To open their eyes, and to turn them from darkness to light, and from the power of Satan unto God, that they may receive forgiveness of sins, and inheritance among them which are sanctified by faith that is in me."

2 Corinthians 5:17 says, "Therefore if any man be in Christ, he is a new creature: old things are passed away; behold all things are become new."

Have you accepted Jesus Christ as your personal savior?

Read Romans 10:9-13

That if thou shalt confess with thy mouth the Lord Jesus, and shalt believe in thine heart that God hath raised him from the dead, thou shalt be saved. For with the heart man believeth unto righteousness; and with the mouth confession is made unto salvation. For the scripture saith, whosoever believeth on him shall not be ashamed. For there is no difference between the Jew and the Greek: for the same Lord over all is rich unto all that call upon him. For whosoever shall call upon the name of the Lord shall be saved.

Write a brief testimony of your salvation.

_____

_____

_____

_____

_____

Do others see Christ in you? It is time to turn the soil. Turn your life away from sin. Most of us have heard the saying, "You may be the only bible some people read." What are people reading in your life? When people look at you and how you live your life as a Christian, do they say or think, 'I wish I were like that' or do they say or think 'If you call that a Christian, leave me out'?

Matthew 5:13-16 says we are to be the salt of the earth and light of the world.
Ye are the salt of the earth: but if the salt have lost his savour, wherewith shall it be salted? it is thenceforth good for nothing, but

to be cast out, and to be trodden under foot of men. Ye are the light of the world. A city that is set on an hill cannot be hid. Neither do men light a candle, and put it under a bushel, but on a candlestick; and it giveth light unto all that are in the house. Let your light so shine before men, that they may see your good works, and glorify your Father which is in heaven.

Do others see the light of Christ in you? In your own words, what do you think people say about you?

_____

_____

_____

_____

_____

Do others see Christ in you? Have you prepared the soil? After the ground has been turned, you run a tiller through the garden to soften the dirt. In life we need to read God's word and pray. After salvation, we should get into a bible believing church and learn God's word. 2 Timothy chapter 4 tells us to be instant in season. As a Christian, we should always be ready to witness to other, to share our testimony and share the Word.

Prepare your soul by putting God's word in your heart. Read God's word daily. Find a bible study at your church or somewhere nearby. I love going to a women's small group Bible study. My husband loves going to men's group Bible studies. It allows them to get to know each other, share their personal experiences and study God's word together.

I love to try to memorize bible verses. As a child our church had a contest where we won prizes for memorizing the most verses. I loved it. I often won prizes too. As a very competitive person, I would have been happy to just be called a winner. As I got older, I started writing verses on post cards and taping them up in places I would see them daily. I put a couple of them on the bathroom mirror and on a mirror in bedroom where I get dressed. Now I put scriptures in my overhead at work.

I used to put scriptures on notes in many different languages at the ends of our machines at work. The Hispanics and the Asians loved it. It really thrilled them that I not only put it in English but put it in their language. Reading Bible scripture throughout the day and going to studies at least one day a week and going to church services 2-3 times a week helps put God's word in your heart. This is one way to till the ground, prepare the soul.

We turned the ground when we accepted Jesus Christ as our Savior. We till the ground when we turn the rich nutrients into our body by putting God's word into our heart. As you continue to read this book, pray and ask God to show you where he wants you to grow. Ask God to help you sow seeds into other's lives.

If you have accepted Christ as your savior then you have turned the soil, however, it is not quite ready for sowing yet. Let's pick out the rocks and glass and any other debris that may be in the way. Consider sins in your life as the rocks, sticks, glass, and thorns.

Matthew 7:3-5
And why beholdest thou the mote that is in thy brother's eye, but considerest not the beam that is in thine own eye? Or how wilt thou

*say to thy brother, Let me pull out the mote out of thine eye; and,
behold, a beam is in thine own eye? Thou hypocrite, first cast out
the beam out of thine own eye; and then shalt thou see clearly to
cast out the mote out of thy brother's eye.*

I like to plow some mushroom dirt into my soil. It is a
fertilizer made of horse manure and hay. Some gardeners use
other manures. It stinks. Running a tiller is not easy. It is back-
breaking and makes me sweat a lot. But I just keep my eyes on
the goal. This is tilled into the garden before time to sow seeds.

When I stay focused on my goal, I can work harder without
even realizing how hard I am really working. I know that the
fertile ground will produce a huge harvest. As we read God's
word, we will learn more of what He has in store for us. It is
not always easy to do the right thing but remember what the
blessing will be, and you can keep on going.

I have heard people say they can't understand the bible.
I suggest you keep reading. Sometimes we try too hard to
understand some details that are not for us yet. Start with a
study of a particular subject, or a bible study with a group. Do
not just stop reading.

I like to pray and ask God to show me what He would
have me learn from a passage. I often write notes. It helps me
to remember when I write it down. When my children were
little, I read a lot of children's bible stories. Then I would read
the passage in the bible that went along with what I was reading
to my kids.

When I began teaching the children's class at my church, I
would read the story, study the passage in the bible and make

notes with study questions. When I got to church, I felt like I really understood what I was reading to my children. When they ask questions, usually I have the answer. Reading the children's bible stories does help to know the story itself, but it does not stop there.

I had done a study of the life of David with my class. It was a good lesson, and I thought I knew the story well. As a few years had passed I was in an adult ladies' bible study that took us into the life of David in a much different view. So even though I did know the story itself, sometimes God wants us to see behind the scenes.

Later as more years went by, in yet another class, I found myself back in the study of David in another perspective. You can look at each character in the story of David and study each person individually. The life of David can take so many different views and we can relate his life with ours at all different levels from childhood to adulthood to wisdom.

There is so much to learn in God's word. You can read it through its entirety over and over again and still learn something new. The example I gave of David is only one of many. Keep reading and studying God's Word. Don't stop at the surface, dig deep. You can learn stories in the Bible. You can learn characters and how God uses them. You can study the history from all the areas in which the Bible was written. There are so many different ways to study the Bible.

You **can** understand the bible. Do not give up. Ask for help. Join a study group. You are a garden. Prepare the soil. It may not always be easy, but the harvest is worth it all. Put God's word in your heart.

Remember you are the garden. Your body is the temple of the Holy Spirit. We should take care of our body. This includes eating right and exercise for physical health. We need to put the right things into our mind and heart for mental and spiritual health.

Galatians 6:9 *And let us not be weary in well doing: for in due season, we shall reap, if we faint not.*

2 Timothy 2:15 *Study to shew thyself approved unto God, a workman that needeth not to be ashamed, rightly dividing the word of truth.*

It has been said that to stop a bad habit, you stop doing it for 21 days and you can break the habit. I have also heard to replace the bad habit you do something else for 21 days. If we would replace sinful things with things that are of God, we can change a bad habit to not just a good thing, but something God could be pleased with. Let's fertilize our garden. Let's make our soil fertile for God. How can we do that? By replacing those sinful things with positive encouraging things.

I have compiled a list of encouraging scriptures. Read through these. Look them up in your bible and study them. These are some good ones to write on postcards and keep handy. Use these as memory verses. These are great memory verses.

Philippians 4:13 *I can do all things through Christ which strengtheneth me.*

Philippians 2:14 *Do all things without murmurings and disputings.*

Philippians 4:8 *Finally, brethren, whatsoever things are true, whatsoever things are honest, whatsoever things are just, whatsoever things are pure, whatsoever things are lovely, whatsoever things are of good report; if there be any virtue, and if there be any praise, think on these things.*

(Staying positive in life can lead to better health.)

Romans 8:28 *And we know that all things work together for good to them that love God, to them who are the called according to his purpose.*

1 Corinthians 10:31 *Whether therefore ye eat, or drink, or whatsoever ye do, do all to the glory of God.*

Colossians 3:23 *And whatsoever ye do, do it heartily, as to the Lord, and not unto men;*

Ephesians 4:26-27 *Be ye angry, and sin not: let not the sun go down upon your wrath: Neither give place to the devil.*

1 Thessalonians 5:17-18 *Pray without ceasing. In every thing give thanks: for this is the will of God in Christ Jesus concerning you.*

2 Thessalonians 3:13 *But ye, brethren, be not weary in well doing.*

Hebrew 4:16 *Let us therefore come boldly unto the throne of grace, that we may obtain mercy, and find grace to help in time of need.*

James 1:2 *My brethren, count it all joy when ye fall into divers temptations;*

Romans 12:12-14 *Rejoicing in hope; patient in tribulation; continuing instant in prayer; Distributing to the necessity of saints; given to hospitality. Bless them which persecute you: bless, and curse not.*

Now I want to look at the fruit of the spirit. You will see these verses in different areas in this book. For now, let's just read through the scriptures.

Galatians 5:22-23 *But the fruit of the Spirit is love, joy, peace, longsuffering, gentleness, goodness, faith, Meekness, temperance: against such there is no law.*

As we add fertilizer to our soil, it is tilled into the ground. This will make the crops grow abundantly. Fertilizer gives the garden the nutrients it needs to allow the vegetables to grow and increase.

We are God's garden. God's Word is the fertilizer. As we put God's Word into our heart, it allows us to be fruitful. We must read the bible daily. The fruit of the spirit are things that we could fill our life with in which there is no law against.

LOVE
JOY
PEACE
LONG-SUFFERING
GENTLENESS
GOODNESS
FAITH
MEEKNESS
TEMPERANCE

We should pray and ask God to fill us with the fruit of the spirit. Study each one and ask yourself where you need to improve. With God's help, we can all be more fruitful. (We will discuss the fruit of the spirit in more detail later in this book.)

2 Timothy 2:15 *Study to shew thyself approved unto God, a workman that needeth not to be ashamed, rightly dividing the word of truth.*

2 Timothy 4:2 *Preach the word; be instant in season, out of season; reprove, rebuke, exhort with all longsuffering and doctrine.*

As we begin to till in the fertilizer (God's Word) into our lives, we realize it is not always easy, but it is always worthwhile. Just like tilling the fertilizer into the garden, sometimes it stinks or is painful. Although I never would say that God's word stinks, the point I want to make is simply that it is not always what we want to hear.

I hope you read all the verses on sin and have realized the stones in your life that need removed. As you begin getting sin out of your life, you need to replace the space with nutrients of God's word. I like to be filled with the 'fruit of the spirit'.

I have already named the fruits and given a brief description of what each one is. As I have mentioned, tilling in the word is not always easy. An example of one fruit that comes to mind is faith. Did you know in order to receive faith you have to go through some trials?

If you never go through trials, how would you ever really know if you truly have faith? It is the going through that is hard. Everyone in the entire world goes through trials. It is certainly easier to handle those trials when you have Jesus Christ to lean on.

How we handle trials says a lot about a person's faith. When we fail the test, we may have to face the same test again. I personally have gone through a lot of trials that afterwords I look back and realize I learned something from it. I may not be able to explain why things happen, but everything happens for a purpose. It may be years later before we know why, or we may never know why.

Think of some trials you went through and explain how it helped you grow your faith.

_____

_____

_____

_____

_____

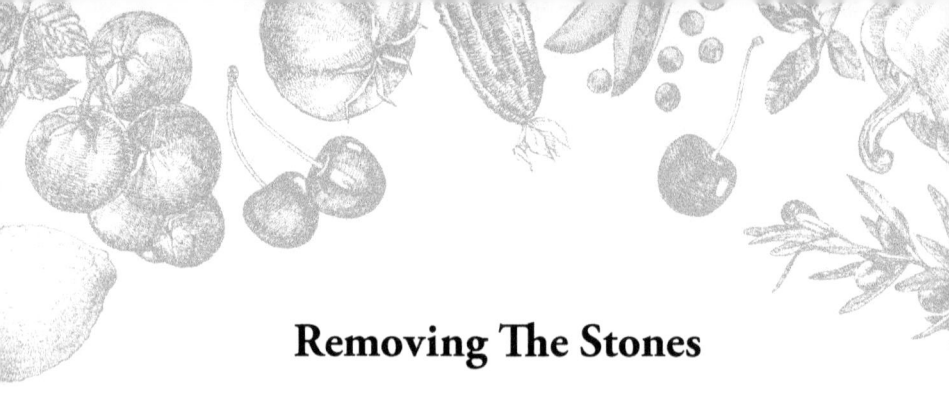

Removing The Stones

Sin can be many things. Some are obvious, while other sins are silent, not so noticeable. We know the ten commandments that tell us not to kill, steal, lie, cheat, or commit adultery. Have you ever studied these and really applied each one to your life? Let's take a look at the ten commandments.

Exodus 20:3-17

Thou shalt have no other gods before me. Thou shalt not make unto thee any graven image, or any likeness of any thing that is in heaven above, or that is in the earth beneath, or that is in the water under the earth:Thou shalt not bow down thyself to them, nor serve them: for I the LORD thy God am a jealous God, visiting the iniquity of the fathers upon the children unto the third and fourth generation of them that hate me; And shewing mercy unto thousands of them that love me, and keep my commandments. Thou shalt not take the name of the LORD thy God in vain; for the LORD will not hold him guiltless that taketh his name in vain. Remember the sabbath day, to keep it holy. Six days shalt thou labour, and do all thy work: But the seventh day is the sabbath of the LORD thy God: in it thou shalt not do any work, thou, nor thy son, nor thy daughter, thy manservant, nor thy maidservant, nor thy cattle, nor thy stranger that is within thy gates: For in six days the LORD made heaven and earth, the sea, and all that in them is, and rested the seventh day: wherefore the LORD blessed the sabbath day, and hallowed it. Honour thy father and thy mother: that thy days may be long upon the land which the LORD thy God giveth thee. Thou shalt not kill.

Thou shalt not bear false witness against thy neighbor. Thou shalt not commit adultery. Thou shalt not steal.
Thou shalt not covet thy neighbor's house, thou shalt not covet thy neighbor's wife, nor his manservant, nor his maidservant, nor his ox, nor his ass, nor any thing that is thy neighbor's.

What things have you put before God?

_____

_____

_____

_____

_____

The First commandment says to have no other gods before God. In general, we may not consider some things we do as having before God, but let's look at some things we do in a different prospective.

We are supposed to worship God and put Him first before anything. So how do we put God first? In our marriage we may put our spouse first by taking into consideration what pleases them. We would do things that make a spouse happy and try not to do things that we know would make them upset. We do that because we love our spouse, and it pleases us, to make our spouse happy. We spend time with our spouse. As we get to know our spouse, we learn more about their likes and dislikes. How would a marriage work if you never spent time together?

In the same aspect we must spend time with God and His word in order to get to know Him. The more we get to know

God the more we can learn what pleases Him. We put God first by spending time with Him in His word and in prayer. The more we do this the more we learn to love God and truly put Him first in our life.

We so often put things before God and do not even realize it is sinful. For example, if you are watching 3 hours of television or on a computer, phone, or Facebook each day, but you do not open God's word or take time to pray, then you may be putting that TV, phone, or computer before God. Maybe you spend two hours in the gym a day and never read God's word. Some people would never miss a football game, but you never see them in a church. None of these things in themselves are wrong, however when you put those things before God, that becomes your god.

Psalm 119:37 *Turn away mine eyes from beholding vanity; and quicken thou me in thy way.*

Put God first before all things. Take time to get to know God's word and what pleases God. Read Matthew 6:33.

Matthew 6:33 *But seek ye first the kingdom of God, and his righteousness; and all these things shall be added unto you.*

Matthew 6:25-34 tells us not to worry so much about our life as far as what we wear or eat. Instead, we should be busy putting God first and He will take care of all the other for us.

Therefore I say unto you, Take no thought for your life, what ye shall eat, or what ye shall drink; nor yet for your body, what ye shall put on. Is not the life more than meat, and the body than raiment? Behold the fowls of the air: for they sow not, neither do they reap, nor gather into barns; yet your heavenly Father feedeth them. Are ye not much better than they? Which of you by taking thought can add one cubit unto his stature? And why take ye thought for raiment? Consider the lilies of the field, how they grow; they toil not, neither do they spin: And yet I say unto you, That even Solomon in all his glory was not arrayed like one of these. Wherefore, if God so clothe the grass of the field, which to day is, and to morrow is cast into the oven, shall he not much more clothe you, O ye of little faith? Therefore take no thought, saying, What shall we eat? or, What shall we drink? or, Wherewithal shall we be clothed? (For after all these things do the Gentiles seek:) for your heavenly Father knoweth that ye have need of all these things. But seek ye first the kingdom of God, and his righteousness; and all these things shall be added unto you. Take therefore no thought for the morrow: for the morrow shall take thought for the things of itself. Sufficient unto the day is the evil thereof.

Let's make sure we have no other god before our almighty God. Keep God first in everything you do.

The Second commandment tells us not to make or worship idols. John 4:24 says God is a spirit and those who worship Him are to worship Him in spirit. Allow Christ to speak to your spirit. Listen to what He is saying to you.

Although we may not bow down and pray to some things in our life, have we allowed our phones or other things to become our idols in our life. We can't leave our homes without that cell phone, but how many of us keep a bible at our side?

You often see teenagers idolizing a young singer. I understand looking up to someone, allowing someone to mentor you or give you encouragement to succeed; however, do not let that become an idol in your life. As technology grows and allows us to see and hear so many others at any time, we tend to listen to our favorite singers which if not careful could turn into an idol.

The Third commandment tells us not to take the name of the Lord our God in vain. God's name should be precious to us and have great meaning. Do not use God's name in cursing. God's name should be sacred. Pay attention to the language of yourself and those around you. Speak up and ask those around you to not use God's name in vein.

The names of God are so precious, yet we have no idea how powerful those names are. Try studying the names of God and each meaning.

Matthew 6:9 (KJV) *After this manner therefore pray ye: Our Father which art in heaven, Hallowed be thy name.*

The Fourth commandment tells us to remember the sabbath and keep it holy. We should set aside one day a week to honor God, by worshiping Him. This is a day we cease work and focus on God and rest. God worked six days and rested on the seventh.

I realize that due to work schedules these days, sometimes we must work on our day of worship or take a chance to lose our jobs. So, I have come up with some ideas that may help. Take your bible and/or a bible study book to work with you. Read and study God's word during your breaks and lunch period. Take time to pray over your food before eating. Do your best to keep the sabbath holy.

Genisis 2:2-3 *And on the seventh day God ended his work which he had made; and he rested on the seventh day from all his work which he had made. And God blessed the seventh day, and* sanctified it: because that in it he had rested from all his work which God created and made.

The Fifth commandment tells us to honor our mother and father. This is the only commandment with promise. Read it. It says if we honor our parents, we can have a long life. Wow!

As an adult, we can still honor our parents. My husband often asks, "How do you spell love?" T-I-M-E. Spend time with your parents if they are still alive. If they have passed, do not be afraid to talk about them. Do things in remembrance of your parents who have passed.

As a grandparent myself, I can promise you time with the grandchildren is the most precious time in the world. This does not mean dumping your kids off on the grandparents to raise. I enjoy one day every other weekend with my four grandchildren. I look forward to this time. This is honorable for me, for my son to allow me this time with my precious grandchildren. Zoom and video chat work great if distance keeps you apart.

Another way to honor one's parents is simply saying thank you for little things. My mother is uneducated and a very slow learner. (mentally slow). We had a birthday party for her one year where I bragged at how she taught me to read simple words and simple math. She taught me and my sibling what she could. I wanted her to know how much I appreciated what she taught me. It was her that groomed me into my love for books.

Honoring your parents is not something we should ever stop doing. We should find ways to honor our parents as long as we live. Say you're sorry, say thank you. Take care of your parents as they become elderly. Love with your time. Visit your parents and spend time with them. Take a parent or grandparent to lunch or dinner. Sit and talk with your parents. Sometimes a simple phone call will make them feel better.

The Sixth commandment says do not murder. Physically speaking this is self-explanatory. However, we could ponder the thought of spiritually killing someone. Hatred, anger, and insults could cause others to not accept Christ as their savior resulting in a spiritual death.

The Seventh says do not commit adultery. This is another one that is self-explanatory. I suggest never allow yourself to be in the situation where this could happen. Never be alone with the opposite sex unless you are married. Always have company to help keep you accountable.

The Eighth says do not steal. No matter how small or large, stealing is stealing. If it does not belong to you, leave it alone.

The Ninth tells us not to lie. No even a little white lie is okay. Lying by omission can get you into trouble as well. Sometimes the truth hurts.

The Tenth tells us to not covet or to not selfishly desire things that do not belong to us. Oh, sometimes I wish I had a large house with in-ground pool and large yard… You understand, right? We should not covet or want things others have. Learn to be content. This does not mean we cannot thrive for more, work hard to have things. But do not go into debt to have what the neighbor has. Do not want or desire things to the point it consumes you.

Psalm 119:36 *Incline my heart unto thy testimonies, and not to covetousness.*

These commandments are there to help us to know what sins are and to help us steer away from sins. There are other sins listed in the bible. We need to know what God's word says about sin. I am listing several scriptures on the next page for you to read. Read through these and allow God to show you if you are living in any sinful way that you need to change and turn away from. Let's get the rocks out of our garden.

What are some stones in your life?

_____

_____

_____

_____

_____

Proverbs 6:16-19 *These six things doth the LORD hate: yea, seven are an abomination unto him: A proud look, a lying tongue, and hands that shed innocent blood, An heart that deviseth wicked imaginations, feet that be swift in running to mischief, A false witness that speaketh lies, and he that soweth discord among brethren.*

Romans 1:24-32 *Wherefore God also gave them up to uncleanness through the lusts of their own hearts, to dishonor their own bodies between themselves: Who changed the truth of God into a lie, and worshiped and served the creature more than the Creator, who is blessed for ever. Amen. For this cause God gave them up unto vile affections: for even their women did change the natural use into that which is against nature: {Homosexuality is a sin.} And likewise also the men, leaving the natural use of the woman, burned in their lust one toward another; men with men working that which is unseemly, and receiving in themselves that* *recompense of their error which was meet. And even as they did not like to retain God in their knowledge, God gave them over to a reprobate mind, to do those things which are not convenient; Being filled with all unrighteousness, fornication, wickedness, covetousness, maliciousness; full of envy, murder, debate, deceit, malignity; whisperers, Backbiters, haters of God, despiteful, proud, boasters, inventors of evil things, disobedient to parents, Without understanding, covenant breakers, without natural affection, implacable, unmerciful: Who knowing the judgment of God, that they which commit such things are worthy of death, not only do the same, but have pleasure in them that do them.*

Romans 12:1 *I beseech you therefore, brethren, by the mercies of God, that ye present your bodies a living sacrifice, holy, acceptable unto God, which is your reasonable service.*

Are you holy?

1 Corinthians 3:16-17 *Know ye not that ye are the temple of God, and that the Spirit of God dwelleth in you? If any man defile the temple of God, him shall God destroy; for the temple of God is holy, which temple ye are.*

Let's take a minute to look at this one. Our body is the temple of the Lord's. **What?** You mean the Spirit of God dwells in my body? Yes, that is what the word of God tells us. So, we should respect our body. In that, not only should we **not** use our body for sin, but we should also take care of our body for God. (We will go into more details on this when we study fertilizing our garden.)

Galatians 5:16-21 *This I say then, Walk in the Spirit, and ye shall not fulfill the lust of the flesh. For the flesh lusteth against the Spirit, and the Spirit against the flesh: and these are contrary the one to the other: so*

24

that ye cannot do the things that ye would. But if ye be led of the Spirit, ye are not under the law. Now the works of the flesh are manifest, which are these; Adultery, fornication, uncleanness, lasciviousness, Idolatry, witchcraft, hatred, variance, emulations, wrath, strife, seditions, heresies, Envyings, murders, drunkenness, revellings, and such like: of the which I tell you before, as I have also told you in time past, that they which do such things shall not inherit the kingdom of God.

Take time to look up the meaning of each of the sins listed here. Ask God to show you what each word means and how it applies to you personally.

Envy, murder, drunkenness, reveling, idolatry, witchcraft, hatred, variance, emulations, wrath, strife, seditions, heresies, adulteries, fornication, uncleanness, lasciviousness.

What kind of rocks, sticks, or other debris is in your garden?

Take time to pray and ask God to show you where you need to change. What are the sins in my life? Are your sins on the surface or are they deeper in the soil? Some rocks are dug out as we plow God's word into our lives.

_____

_____

_____

_____

_____

We have now turned and plowed the soil. We picked out some stones, sticks, and other things hindering us from a bountiful garden. Now let's get ready for some seeds.

Sowing Seeds

Now that we have turned the soil, removed the stones, and added the fertilizer to the garden, we are now ready to sow seeds. Every time we speak the Word, we are sowing seeds. God's word is the seeds. There are many ways to sow seeds. Preaching, reading, singing, and speaking the Word are the most common seeds.

If we study God's word daily, we can be ready to teach, preach, or just testify, and live our lives as God would have us to live. When our light shines, we stand out. This causes people to notice something different about us. They often ask us, "how do you handle that?", or "wish I were more like that" or "where do you go to church?" These statements are opportunities to 'plant seeds'.

As I said at the beginning of this book, we are so often the only bible some people read. We are to be the light of the world and the salt of the earth. We do not have to wear t-shirts that say look at me I am a Christian. (Although that can help be a conversation starter and help lead people to Christ.) If we have the fruits of the spirit in us, we will stand out in a good way. People notice the kindness about us. There will be a peace that only comes from God.

For over twelve years I worked in childcare. I often took care of ten to twelve children at a time. I loved it and was usually happy and cheerful. I had a few people to ask me what I took to be able to handle that many kids? I explained I did not take anything. It was a peace that comes from Jesus Christ. This was planting a seed.

In the parable of sowing seeds, Jesus talks about seeds falling on stony ground, or in the thorns. We can sow seeds everywhere we go. Although in a garden, we do try to sow the seeds in the rows we dug, often seeds will still fall onto the sides of the row. You can read this in Luke 8:4-15.

In life, those stony and thorny places may be in areas we used to live a sinful life ourselves. For example, maybe you use to drink, party, or use drugs. Now that you are saved and trying to plant seeds into the lives of your past peers, they hear what you say, but they do not go to church or may not be around other Christians to encourage them to live right. So, in turn, they do not grow in the Word and quickly wither away.

Also, you may have witnessed to a peer, co-worker, or friend, and they do accept Christ as their Savior. Maybe they go to church a few times and read a little while. However, they did not turn away from their sinful life. They still hang around the other people that they use too. They still have worldly people around them. They do not separate themselves from the world. In turn, they get choked out by the world. They too, turn back to their sinful ways.

This is why it is so important to turn away from sin. We must separate ourselves from the things that are not of God. We must put godly people in our life and spend time reading God's Word. Fill our life with things that are not of the world, but of God. In a garden if you do not keep weeds out, they can choke out the new growth.

1 John 2:15-17 *Love not the world, neither the things that are in the world. If any man love the world, the love of the Father is not in him. For all that is in the world, the lust of the flesh, and the lust of the eyes, and the pride of life, is not of the Father, but is of the world. And the world passeth away, and the lust thereof: but he that doeth the will of God abideth for ever.*

Romans 12:2 *And be not conformed to this world: but be ye transformed by the renewing of your mind, that ye may prove what is that good, and acceptable, and perfect, will of God.*

Ephesians 4:22-32 *That ye put off concerning the former conversation the old man, which is corrupt according to the deceitful lusts; And be renewed in the spirit of your mind; And that ye put on the new man, which after God is created in righteousness and true holiness. Wherefore putting away lying, speak every man truth with his neighbour: for we are members one of another. Be ye angry, and sin not: let not the sun go down upon your wrath: Neither give place to the devil. Let him that stole steal no more: but rather let him labour, working with his hands the thing which is good, that he may have to give to him that needeth. Let no corrupt communication proceed out of your mouth, but that which is good to the use of edifying, that it may minister grace unto the hearers. And grieve not the holy Spirit of God, whereby ye are sealed unto the day of redemption. Let all bitterness, and wrath, and anger, and clamour, and evil speaking, be put away from you, with all malice: And be ye kind one to another, tenderhearted, forgiving one another, even as God for Christ's sake hath forgiven you.*

Ephesians 5:7-11 *Be not ye therefore partakers with them. For ye were sometimes darkness, but now are ye light in the Lord: walk as children of light: (For the fruit of the Spirit is in all goodness and righteousness and truth;) Proving what is acceptable unto the Lord.*

And have no fellowship with the unfruitful works of darkness, but rather reprove them.

We must try to encourage all new believers to go to church and read God's word daily. We do not want them to wither away or be choked out by other sinners. We want them to grow and produce more fruit.

Sow seeds throughout your life. Everywhere we go and everything we do we are sowing seeds. Let God's light shine through your life. Let others see the joy of Christ in you. Do all things as if doing it for God. Do all thing without complaining.

Philippians 2:13-14 *For it is God which worketh in you both to will and to do of his good pleasure. Do all things without murmurings and disputings:*

1 Corinthians 10:31 *Whether therefore ye eat, or drink, or whatsoever ye do, do all to the glory of God.*

As we go through life we can sow seeds daily. Everywhere we go we interact with people; we can sow seeds. 1Corinthians 13:13 says the greatest of these is Love. We can show love to everyone around us by being friendly and compassionate. I call this sowing seeds of love. We should not show judgement or be hateful to people just because we disagree or have different beliefs. A little kindness can go a long way.

An example of sowing seeds of love can be working with people of different backgrounds or beliefs than your own. Instead of judging or arguing about what you believe is right, share your belief and let them share theirs. Remain friendly and invite them to church. Show kindness and love to everyone.

My husband had saw an elderly lady and her grown son walking to town and he noticed her shoes were worn. The soles were literally flopping. He wanted to buy her some shoes but had not seen her again for a while. As he and I were out one day, we saw them out. We pulled over and asked her shoe size. We went to a local store and bought her a pair of shoes and took them to her. Her and her son were so happy. This is sowing seeds of kindness.

My husband had received a small jar containing a mustard seed in it. We knew what it was and what it represented. I hung it on the rear-view mirror of my car. Soon we started talking about ordering some tiny jars and making those to give out. We started with 50 jars, then 100 and another 100. We have now given out over 500 of these mustard seed jars. I went a step further by printed in both English and Spanish Matthew 17:20 on small cardstock to drop in the snack zip bags we put the jars with stretchy string. They can be worn as a necklace or hung in an area to remind you to have faith. We have heard testimonies as little as a simple "thank you, I needed that" to "you have no idea what this means to me, I was about to give up…".

I call this our mustard seed ministry. Everywhere we go now, we keep a few of these little snack bags containing the scripture cards and the jar with the mustard seed on a stretchy cord. We pray that God will show us any time we should give it to a person. Sometimes it is at the gas pumps when the person across from us speaks to us and we feel led to give one. Sometimes it is at work or at the grocery store. It almost always opens the door to conversation about Christ. We very seldom get told no. Most people accept the gift. The mustard seed ministry is a way of sowing seeds of Faith.

We have talked about sowing seeds of love, kindness and faith. When we have cultivated our own life with the word of God. We have learned God's word and have it hidden in our heart. Never be ashamed to speak up and share God's word. Be kind and show love to everyone around you. Share your testimony to others to help others have faith. The seed inside us should show up on the outside of us.

What kind of seeds are you sowing?

_____

_____

_____

_____

Water, Sun, and Fertilize

To begin with, as we get ready to plant our garden, it must be the right season. It must be after the last frost and warm weather. God gave us seasons for everything. Spring is the season for sowing. Summer is the season for growing. Fall is the season for harvest. Winter is the season of rest.

As we plant seeds, we must immediately water the garden. As the plants begin to grow, we want to fertilize the garden but be careful not to over fertilize. You can burn the new plants up by over fertilizing. We also continue to pull weeds from the garden. Sometimes weeds are too close to the plant to pull out without disturbing the root of the plant, so you let it grow with the plant. If possible, you can cut the top of the weed without disturbing the plant.

In my life, I had a great husband, with the best marriage in the world. I went to church all the time and taught Sunday school etc. My husband only went to church occasionally yet encouraged me to stay in church and live right. He often watched movies that had cursing in them that I personally felt was a weed in the root in which I could not quiet pluck. So, I clipped the top by going into other rooms, cleaning, or reading.

Each year as we would till a fertilizer into the garden between the rows. We were careful not to get it on the plants themselves. We only wanted it between the rows. The roots of the crop would draw nourishment from this without burning it. Also, Turning the ground allows oxygen into the soil. As nutrients are used in the sowing season, we must re-nourish in the growing season.

God showed me that this is like when we have led someone to the Lord, we get them to go to church and get baptized. Then we allow them to feed off our fertile life. We do not have to preach or hound them every second of the day. They must grow over time. It takes time with water, sun, feeding and weeding to grow into a fruitful plant.

Watering the crop may come from God in the form of rain or we ourselves may have to water. Some people allow God to minister to them in the form of reading the Word themselves or listening to preachers. However, some people don't get grounded into a church and we must water them by being witnesses or testifying. Allow others to see Christ in you.

As I worked in a manufacturing plant, we were allowed to listen to radios at our workstations. I always listen to gospel. Also, if anyone cursed in my presence, I politely ask them to please not use that language in front of me. Amazingly, everyone there was extremely respectful to me. I was always friendly, kind and kept a smile on my face as I spoke to others about not wanting to hear the language. My kindness was returned with kindness and respect.

Very quickly word got out through the plant that Sarah was a Christian. Soon people would come to me to ask questions about the bible or clarification of something they did not understand. Some questions would be where in the bible is ... or what does the bible say about... If I did not know the answer, I would search for it and get them the answer usually by the next day.

We are the fertilizer for the new Christians that are around us. I did not go around saying I'm a Christian. I just lived a life that others could see Christ in me. God used me to help others. I became close friends with a few other Christians that were of other denominations. We respected each other's beliefs. We all agreed on the one living God and Jesus Christ as our Savior. It was our kindness, generosity, and loving spirit that fed those around us.

At another manufacturing plant I worked at a few years later, we were not allowed to have radios. Those around me did quickly learn I was a Christian. When someone would ask me how my weekend was, I would tell all about the wonderful service we had at church. (planting seeds) There was always something exciting going on at our church. I was also the youth leader, so often I would tell what our youth was doing. I went to church every Sunday morning and night and Wednesday night. So, I always had a church service to talk about.

I usually got to work early and made a round through the production line to greet and cheer up all the former shift. I was always happy, cheerful, and joyous. If a co-worker was in a bad mood, I would listen to the problem and usually would find something positive to tell them about what was going on. By the time I walked away from that person, usually they were smiling. Sunshine can be our smiles and friendliness.

I also would know what was going on with the production from that shift. I was able to use the time to learn about the job while spreading the joy of the Lord at the same time. I did the same thing at the end of my shift. I would go around with a cheerful hello; hope you have a great day while letting them know about the production. Sowing seeds of hope. Find ways everywhere you go to sow those seeds.

In my life as I worked, I tried to maintain a positive attitude. Even if I did not totally love my job, I had the attitude, I must work to live so I might as well enjoy it while I am here. I also prayed for God to use me wherever I worked. If you are a willing vessel, God can and will use you. We should allow our life to reflect God's love. This can be the water, sun and fertilizer to help others around us grow in Christ. We would then be producing fruit.

What do you do that may be fertilizing or watering?

_____

_____

_____

_____

_____

Philippians 4:8 *Finally, brethren, whatsoever things are true, whatsoever things are honest, whatsoever things are just, whatsoever things are pure, whatsoever things are lovely, whatsoever things are of good report; if there be any virtue, and if there be any praise, think on these things.*

Philippians 2:14 *Do all things without murmurings and disputings:*

1 Corinthians 10:31 *Whether therefore ye eat, or drink, or whatsoever ye do, do all to the glory of God.*

In all things we do, we should do it as if we were doing it for God. I must work so instead of complaining about it, I learned to enjoy my job and use it as a place to witness to others. God has blessed me so much in every place that I've worked. I know I'm doing what God would have me to do when others come to me for prayer request and ask questions. Those are conformations that I am where God wants me to be.

God has called each of us to a holy calling. Some are to be preachers, teachers, deacons, singers, witnesses, encourages, and many other types of water or fertilizer. Let's allow God to work through our lives. Let the light of Christ shine in your life. Do others see Christ in you? I pray daily that others can see His light through me.

2 Timothy 1:9 *Who hath saved us, and called us with an holy calling, not according to our works, but according to his own purpose and grace, which was given us in Christ Jesus before the world began.*

Everyone is not to be like me. You may have a whole different personality than I do, so you may not be able to go around with a cheerful, positive attitude that God has blessed me with. Maybe God has blessed you with a powerful, leadership, controlling type personality. God can use that also for His glory. My pastor is a rather straight forward, tell it like it is kind of person. We love and respect him so much. We know he will not allow us to get by with a sinful life.

Every person has their own personality. God has given each of us a different personality to make up the body of Christ. Some are the feet, the arms, the eyes, or other parts. We are all needed to make up the whole body. Our lady who cleans the church and decorates the flower arrangements is very quiet and many people have no idea what she does. She is in the background and not seen much, but it is her work that makes our visits to the church so nice. Same thing with the ones who control the sound system. They are quiet but have a huge impact.

I like to think of the sun as the Son. This is messages we get in our heart, directly from God. Just like I feel in my heart as I garden how these little things relate to our spiritual life. As I was picking stones and sticks out of the garden, I felt like God was telling me this is like getting sin out of our life. The stones and sticks can prevent the roots from growing deep, so we must get them out. Let God be the sun in your life.

We need to continue to water, fertilize and soak up the sun of Christ in our daily walk. We need to feed our soul by reading God's word, praying, listen to preaching and gospel music. Allow others to help us to grow while we help others to grow as well. Never stop studying and learning no matter how old you are or what degrees you have. There is always more to learn.

Read **Romans chapter 12**.

I beseech you therefore, brethren, by the mercies of God, that ye present your bodies a living sacrifice, holy, acceptable unto God, which is your reasonable service. And be not conformed to this world: but be ye transformed by the renewing of your mind, that ye may prove what is that good, and acceptable, and perfect, will of God. For I say, through the grace given unto me, to every man that is among you, not to think of himself more highly than he ought to think; but to think soberly, according as God hath dealt to every man the measure of faith. For as we have many members in one body, and all members have not the same office: So we, being many, are one body in Christ, and every one members one of another. Having then gifts differing according to the grace that is given to us, whether prophecy, let us prophesy according to the proportion of faith; Or ministry, let us wait on our ministering: or he that teacheth, on teaching; Or he that exhorteth, on exhortation: he that giveth, let him do it with simplicity; he that ruleth, with diligence; he that sheweth mercy, with cheerfulness. Let love be without dissimulation. Abhor that which is evil; cleave to that which is good. Be kindly affectioned one to another with brotherly love; in honour preferring one another; Not slothful in business; fervent in spirit; serving the Lord; Rejoicing in hope; patient in tribulation; continuing instant in prayer; Distributing to the necessity of saints; given to hospitality. Bless them which persecute you: bless, and curse not. Rejoice with them that do rejoice, and weep with them that weep. Be of the same mind one toward another. Mind not high things, but condescend to men of low estate. Be not wise in your own conceits. Recompense to no man evil for evil. Provide things honest in the sight of all men. If it be possible, as much as lieth in you, live peaceably with all men. Dearly beloved, avenge not yourselves, but rather give place unto wrath: for it is written, Vengeance is mine; I will repay, saith the Lord. Therefore if thine enemy hunger, feed him; if he thirst, give him drink: for in so doing thou shalt heap coals of fire on his head. Be not overcome of evil, but overcome evil with good.

If you are not already using your daily life as a witness for the Lord, ask God how you can witness for Him. Even if you are not allowed to read your bible at work, there are ways to be a witness. Purposely look for ways you can witness to those around you.

What can you do in your daily routine that will magnify the Lord?

_____

_____

_____

_____

_____

Weeding

At the same time, we are fertilizing and watering our garden, the weeds also continue growing. If you have ever planted a garden, you know how the weeds continue to grow throughout the whole season. At the beginning you can plow between the rows, and hoe near your plants. Then the plants get too big to plow between rows, so you can only hoe or hand pull the weeds. As long as you keep most of the weeds out, the garden will flourish and produce a lot of fruit.

This is the same with our life. Even as we grow as Christians, the world is still around us. There will be sin near our life that we can easily remove or get away from. Other sin may just be too close to get away from, so we must keep feeding our spirit with the Word so that sin will not choke us out. We must keep sin out of our life.

For example, when we get saved, we know to not go to bars, do drugs, etc. If a person gets saved, but the spouse does not get saved, you may not be able to get all sin out of your life. However, you can continue to live your life in front of your spouse to win them over. This is the same with a brother or sister or other family member. These people will still be in your life. We are to continue to love them. We must pray for them and witness to them. However, we do not want to join them in their sinful living. (No thanks, I do not do that anymore. I gave my life to Jesus.)

1 Corinthians 7:13-16 *And the woman which hath an husband that believeth not, and if he be pleased to dwell with her, let her not leave him. For the unbelieving husband is sanctified by the wife, and the unbelieving wife is sanctified by the husband: else were your children unclean; but now are they holy. For what knowest thou, O wife, whether thou shalt save thy husband? or how knowest thou, O man, whether thou shalt save thy wife?*

John 15:19 *If ye were of the world, the world would love his own: but because ye are not of the world, but I have chosen you out of the world, therefore the world hateth you.*

John 17:14-15 *I have given them thy word; and the world hath hated them, because they are not of the world, even as I am not of the world. I pray not that thou shouldest take them out of the world, but that thou shouldest keep them from the evil.*

It is so important when we get saved to remember where we came from. We are not to judge others. Instead, we are to love them. We do however need to get as much sin away from our life as we can. God puts a desire in our heart to want to learn more about Him. The more we learn about Christ the more we please Him. God wants to bless us. It is up to us how much blessing we want.

Leviticus 22:31 *Therefore shall ye keep my commandments, and do them: I am the LORD.*

John 14:15 *If ye love me, keep my commandments*

John 15:10-11 *If ye keep my commandments, ye shall abide in my love; even as I have kept my Father's commandments, and abide in his love. These things have I spoken unto you, that my joy might remain in you, and that your joy might be full.*

As we get closer to God, we learn more and more about the blessings God has. People around us respect us more if we live a life that is truly pleasing to God. However, if your life at home is different than our life at church, you will lose respect around you. It is important to be true and honest with yourself and those around you. Do not be a hypocrite or you will lose the trust of those around you. We are not perfect, and we should admit when we are wrong and let those around us know we are also human, and we do make mistakes. God can forgive us and so can those around us.

When I taught Sunday school, I often had teens from my church to visit my house. I did not have to change radio stations or flip channels on the television. Nor did I have to hide magazines. I always listened to gospel music. I read the Bible, Christian commentaries, or other biblically based books. I am not a perfect Christian, nor will I ever be, but I strive to live a life pleasing to my Lord and savior. I want my life to be a life that will help others, not hinder others.

Galatians 5:16-21 *This I say then, Walk in the Spirit, and ye shall not fulfil the lust of the flesh. For the flesh lusteth against the Spirit, and the Spirit against the flesh: and these are contrary the one to the other: so that ye cannot do the things that ye would. But if ye be led of the Spirit, ye are not under the law. Now the works of the flesh are manifest, which are these; Adultery, fornication, uncleanness, lasciviousness, Idolatry, witchcraft, hatred, variance, emulations, wrath, strife, seditions, heresies, Envyings, murders, drunkenness, reveling, and such like: of the which I tell you before, as I have also told you in time past, that they which do such things shall not inherit the kingdom of God.*

As years went by, I taught the teenagers' class. I ask the question, if you knew Jesus was coming to your house in person today, 'what would you need to change?' Think about that. A lot of us wouldn't want the pastor of our church to drop by unexpectedly. Well, Jesus is even more important. He sees you every day and knows everything you do. Let's get the weeds out of our life.

What in your life might be considered as weeds?

_____

_____

_____

_____

_____

John 7:4 *For there is no man that doeth any thing in secret, and he himself seeketh to be known openly. If thou do these things, shew thyself to the world.*

Just the other day, I was pulling weeds out of my flower garden. I realized how easy the younger smaller weeds were to pull. However, the weeds that had been there awhile, were extremely hard to pull. Some weeds I could not even get out without disturbing the roots of my plants.

Psalm 101:8 *I will early destroy all the wicked of the land; that I may cut off all wicked doers from the city of the LORD.*

God showed me through that, the same was true in life. We must get sin out of our life before the roots get entangled in our life. When we stay in sin too long, we become numb to it. It seems to be just part of our life. Get sin out as soon as you know it is there. We have heard sin will take you further than you want to go, keep you longer than you want to stay and cost you more than you want to pay. This is very true. It is like a web that gets you entangled and hard to get out of.

Also, remember to rely on God. We cannot do it alone. It is only through the power of God that we can do anything. We are not able to defeat sin alone. We must pray daily and renew our faith through Jesus Christ in order to overcome sin. We are not able to overcome sin alone. Having a friend as an accountability partner is a great help.

Philippians 4:13 *I can do all things through Christ which strengtheneth me.*

Name a time in your life when sin took you further than you wanted to go?

_____

_____

_____

What kinds of things could be weeds in our life? Weeds can take root in our garden. They can choke out our plants. If it is draining you of your spiritual energy, it is a weed. Negativity is one example of a weed. A family member of mine is always talking negatively about others. I cannot get this family member totally out of my life so what I try to do is tell this person, today is a good day we are not going to talk negatively. When I hear this person starting to talk negatively, I say, hold it, today is a happy day, we are talking about cheerful things. We will change the subject to a positive happier memory.

Political drama can drain life out of us. It can be weeds in our life as well. We need to know about the candidates during any election season, but the negative ads can drain us and make us think only negative things as well. I try to listen to the debates and things where they talk about what they can do or have done for the city, County or nation, so I can make a decision based on that and not drain my life from the negative drama.

In some cases, social media could be a weed in your life. Are you spending hours on social media and getting tied up watching videos or seeing what others have posted or how many likes you have? What about video games? Do you spend hours playing games when you could be learning more about God and His word? It is not that any of these things alone are sinful; however, they can become the weeds that choke out life in us. Do not let these things overtake our lives to the point you are not producing fruit.

What about pornography? Have you become hooked on pornography? You may think it does not hurt anything; it is only you all by yourself. No one will know. God knows. Have you heard the saying once seen, it cannot be unseen? This sin can choke out your fruit by not allowing you to witness to others. Your mind always goes to these sinful thoughts instead of to the love God has for you. This is weed that will choke you. You cannot grow and prosper in God's word while living in sin.

There are many things in this world that may not be sin but when they are not used to glorify God, they can become weeds. I love to spend time with my grandchildren, travel, cook and make crafts. If I do not find ways to glorify God in these hobbies and family times, they can become weeds. Let's work on getting the weeds out of our life and let everything we do glorify our Lord. Stay tunes for *Listening to God through Aprons*.

Pests

As the crop begins to grow, often there are pests that try to eat the vegetables. We sometimes spray or sprinkle a pesticide on the crop that will kill the bugs and not harm the vegetables. If we do not get rid of the bugs, they will eat the crop. Bugs can destroy an entire crop. Allow the Word to be the pesticide.

In our lives, bugs can be people that are always trying to get us to do things that are not right in God's eye. An example that comes to my mind is in the workplace. A preacher worked with a group of guys that loved telling dirty jokes. He never told any, however he did listen and laugh with the other men. When I was looking for this pastor of a church we sometime visited, I ask a co-worker where "preacher" was. (That is what my family always called him.) He had no idea the man was even a preacher.

The co-worker was the one telling me about the action. The jokes were the pests. Although the preacher did not tell the jokes, his testimony was destroyed by allowing the bugs in his life. The people around him had no idea he was a Christian let alone a preacher. The co-worker knew the man did not curse, but he had never commented on their behavior, nor had he ever witnessed to them, so the co-worker had no idea he was a preacher.

Everyone we are around may not respect us as Christians, but we must let our light shine. Even if you are not a preacher, deacon, or teacher, you still need to live your life so others can see Christ in you. We can lead others to Christ by the life we live. We do not have to judge others but letting those around us know that we do not want to be a part of that lifestyle shows respect for ourselves and for God.

Negative thinking can be a weed or a pest as well. God tells us in His word to think on positive things. If we are always looking at what bad things could be, we sow negative seeds. If we look at the positive things in life, we sow positive seeds. Let's try to think more positively.

Philippians 4:8 *Finally, brethren, whatsoever things are true, whatsoever things are honest, whatsoever things are just, whatsoever things are pure, whatsoever things are lovely, whatsoever things are of good report; if there be any virtue, and if there be any praise, think on these things.*

I always planted corn in my garden every year. If we did not spray insecticide on the corn, worms would get inside and eat away at the ears of the corn. From the outside the corn looked fine. You wouldn't know the worms were there until you peel away the shucks. Those big grub worms are always on top.

The worms inside would be the sinful things we do in secret. Sometimes people do things they know are wrong in secret. As long as others do not see them in public, they think it is okay. However, those sins eat away at our soul. An example that comes to mind is pornography. There are people that watch pornography in the privacy of their homes, but it is in their hearts eating away.

There are many other pests that could be eating at your spirit. Some other things that come to my mind are addictions to gambling, drugs, alcohol, sexual sins, or eating disorders. Pests can be anything that takes away your fruitfulness. Pest eat away slowly. We often do not realize we have a problem until it is almost too late.

What kind of pest do you have in your life?

_____

_____

_____

_____

_____

How do we get the pest out of our lives? I firmly believe that prayer is the pesticides in our spiritual life. When Satin comes nipping on me, I pray. Prayer is the most powerful tool we have. God allows us to communicate directly to Him through prayer. We could also have an accountability partner.

Proverbs 15:29 *The LORD is far from the wicked: but he heareth the prayer of the righteous.*

James 5:16 *Confess your faults one to another, and pray one for another, that ye may be healed. The effectual fervent prayer of a righteous man availeth much.*

We must learn to rely on Jesus Christ when mental stress enters our life. Mental stress is a pest that hinders our faith. Most people keep this one inside and try to overcome it alone. We often think if we do not tell others we can find our own way out of the depression. This can be a pest. We must pray and have faith to believe that Christ will answer our prayer. Seek help from professionals and share with your church family as most will walk beside you through the battle. You do not have to walk the path alone.

Matthew 17:20 *And Jesus said unto them, Because of your unbelief: for verily I say unto you, If ye have faith as a grain of mustard seed, ye shall say unto this mountain, Remove hence to yonder place; and it shall remove; and nothing shall be impossible unto you.*

Other pests could be things that corrupt our minds. It can be things we do not even realize are wrong. Examples are the books we read, magazines we look at, movies we watch, or music we listen to. If we do not curse or allow others in our home to curse, why do we allow our TV programs to use such language. Are the books and magazines we read or music we listen to putting thoughts in our minds that we do not need in there?

I had a bible-school teacher one year when I was a teenager who taught about what we listen to. She had asked everyone to bring in the lyrics of any song we liked. She told us it did not matter what kind of song it was. If we listened to rock, country or anything we liked. Bring in the lyrics. She did not tell us why, but we all brought in the lyrics of our favorite songs. She read through several lyrics and explained to us what the author/singer was saying in these songs. They were almost all sexual in content. These songs we listen to can be pests which we do not even realize are eating at our soul from the inside out.

Some of us women love romance movies or books. These could be pests in our lives. I love to read. I can get so wrapped up in a good novel, I do not want to put it down. I have gotten hooked on some Christian romance novels. The stories are incredibly good and very Christian based. They relate real life to Christians and talk about the Bible and the right way to live. There is absolutely nothing wrong with these books. However, when you let them take over your reading of God's word and study of what God wants us to learn, it can become a pest.

I work with a lot of people who love sports. My husband and I love to watch our state's football games. There is nothing wrong with the sport itself. A little healthy competition can be great. However, we cannot let it overtake our life or become a pest. If we could get just as excited about Jesus as we do our favorite sport team, how blessed we could be. Do not let sports become a pest. We must have balance in our life.

Matthew 15:11-18 *Not that which goeth into the mouth defileth a man; but that which cometh out of the mouth, this defileth a man. Then came his disciples, and said unto him, Knowest thou that the Pharisees were offended, after they heard this saying? But he answered and said, Every plant, which my heavenly Father hath not planted, shall be rooted up. Let them alone: they be blind leaders of the blind. And if the blind lead the blind, both shall fall into the ditch. Then answered Peter and said unto him, Declare unto us this parable. And Jesus said, Are ye also yet without understanding? Do not ye yet understand, that whatsoever entereth in at the mouth goeth into the belly, and is cast out into the draught? But those things which proceed out of the mouth come forth from the heart; and they defile the man. For out of the heart proceed evil thoughts, murders, adulteries, fornications, thefts, false witness, blasphemies: These are the things which defile a man: but to eat with unwashen hands defileth not a man. Then Jesus went thence, and departed into the coasts of Tyre and Sidon.*

We would not put poison into our body, yet we allow our heart to be filled with some of the vilest deadliest kinds of poison. What kind of thoughts are you putting into your mind that get into your heart and come out of our mouth?

_____

_____

_____

_____

_____

Psalms 101:2-8 *I will behave myself wisely in a perfect way. O when wilt thou come unto me? I will walk within my house with a perfect heart. I will set no wicked thing before mine eyes: I hate the work of them that turn aside; it shall not cleave to me. A froward heart shall depart from me: I will not know a wicked person. Whoso privily slandereth his neighbour, him will I cut off: him that hath an high look and a proud heart will not I suffer. Mine eyes shall be upon the faithful of the land, that they may dwell with me: he that walketh in a perfect way, he shall serve me. He that worketh deceit shall not dwell within my house: he that telleth lies shall not tarry in my sight. I will early destroy all the wicked of the land; that I may cut off all wicked doers from the city of the LORD.*

Sometimes we have to **prune** our plants. You do this more with the flower gardens, and in house plants than with vegetable gardens. There may be a branch that has dead leaves or rotten fruit on it. These are called sucker branches. They will suck the life out of the plant and cause the whole plant to die. Therefore, we must clip the dead heads off to allow the plant to nourish the fruits.

In life these sucker branches could be people in our life who complain all the time. We must limit our time with these kinds of people, or they will bring us down with them. We ourselves may be the ones who are always complaining. Always being negative will drain life out of us. Same with our pet peeves. Maybe it's our language. We must prune bad words or negative thinking out of our life. Let's get pest out of our life.

We have spent some time talking about things that could become pests in our lives, now let's talk about how to prevent them from being pests. There must be a balance of things in our lives. There is a time and place for everything. We need to set a time aside daily for studying God's word. My husband loves to listen to podcasts daily on his way to and from work, in the shower and while mowing the lawn. I love to listen to gospel music all the time. We both read a little bit every day. We read one chapter together every night before we go to bed.

We all have different lifestyles and times which we can use for learning and studying. When my boys were young, they played sports, and we were busy all the time. I taught Sunday School, so I had no choice but to be prepared. I realized I had to plan time to read and study. We so often let time just whiz by without realizing how much time we waste. God's word is a pesticide. We must put God's word in our mind and heart in order to overcome the pests in our life.

When we make time for God, He becomes the shield that protects us from sin and destruction. We can read Psalm 91 to learn how God can protect us from the enemy. Think of God as our protector. He alone can shield us from the pests that life can throw at us. Never say, "I do not have time." We all have time, we must make time to read, pray and study. Get the word of God in your heart to help shield you from the sins of life.

Read Psalm 91.

What is a pest in your life? And how can you overcome it?

_____

_____

_____

_____

_____

_____

_____

_____

_____

The Fruit

We have prepared the soil, fertilized the ground, sowed the seeds, watered, and fertilized the garden, weeded the garden, and now the crop is growing. The plants begin to produce and multiply. If we continue to water, and weed the garden, it continues to produce.

If you have ever planted a garden, you've probably planted cucumbers. From a distance, you do not see the cucumber plants. However, they are growing quickly. Cucumbers continue to produce more and more as long as you keep them picked. They climb over a large area of ground and the cucumbers themselves are hidden under the leaves. Sometimes they get too big to eat, however they are full of seeds.

Some Christians are like the cucumbers. You do not see them from a distance. They are not teachers, preachers, or deacons. However, they are always in the church. They seem to be everywhere. They help a lot behind the scenes. It could be the people who plan the church plays or vacation bible schools, the janitors, and others in the church who help keep things going. It may be a person who is just so kind, loving, caring, and faithful they reach a lot of people. They help lead many people to Christ by the life they live and the things they cause to happen. They produce a lot of fruit.

Corn is the tallest vegetable in the garden. You can see it from a distance. Some Christians are like the corn. They stand tall and are very well noticed. It sometimes doesn't seem like they produce a whole lot of fruit. They only have about two or three ears of corn per stalk. However, every ear is full of seeds. Do not give up because you do not see a lot of fruit. You may be producing a lot of seeds. This could be the teachers or deacons.

Have you ever picked okra? Oh my, that is the most painful vegetable in the garden. Okra is always the last vegetable in the garden to come up. Then you must cut the lower leaves off. They are kind of prickly. I may be just allergic, but the okra itches me so bad I can't stand it. The itch is deep in the skin. Seems like it itches to the bone. It's nearly unbearable. Oh, but fried okra is good and so good for you. Like the cucumber, the more you pick, the more they produce.

Some Christians are like the okra. They tell you the truth even if it hurts to the core. We do not like it when we are told something we do is wrong. It is painful sometimes to give up things that our flesh really enjoys. The reward in the end will make it worthwhile. The pastor or preacher is like the okra; sometimes the message they give, pricks us to the bone. It is not always fun to hear the truth; however, if we listen to God's word, we can learn and turn from sin.

Galatians 5:16-25 *This I say then, Walk in the Spirit, and ye shall not fulfil the lust of the flesh. For the flesh lusteth against the Spirit, and the Spirit against the flesh: and these are contrary the one to the other: so that ye cannot do the things that ye would. But if ye be led of the Spirit, ye are not under the law. Now the works of the flesh are manifest, which are these; Adultery, fornication, uncleanness, lasciviousness, Idolatry, witchcraft, hatred, variance,* *emulations, wrath, strife, seditions, heresies, Envyings, murders, drunkenness, revellings, and such like: of the which I tell you before, as I have also told you in time past, that they which do such things shall not inherit the kingdom of God. But the fruit of the Spirit is love, joy, peace, longsuffering, gentleness, goodness, faith, Meekness, temperance: against such there is no law. And they that are Christ's have crucified the flesh with the affections and lusts. If we live in the Spirit, let us also walk in the Spirit.*

One year I had a very nice-looking garden. Everything was growing and full of vegetables. My squash plants were beautiful and produced plenty of squash. However, one plant, although it looked really good and was producing squash, it was a bad plant. The squash on that one plant were small, hard, and deep orange. Squash is supposed to be yellow. They get that deep orange look when they stay on the vine too long and get too big. After picking off the bad squash several times and it continued producing bad squash, I finally picked the entire plant and threw it out of the garden.

As I was throwing the plant out, God showed me how sometimes after giving people several opportunities to be fruitful, they still do not obey. He can decide to take them out. God tells us in His word not to be unequally yoked and not to be transformed to the world. He tells us to be fruitful. God's word says you will know them by their fruit.

1 Corinthians 3:16-17 *Know ye not that ye are the temple of God, and that the Spirit of God dwelleth in you? If any man defile the temple of God, him shall God destroy; for the temple of God is holy, which temple ye are.*

2 Corinthians 6:14 *Be ye not unequally yoked together with unbelievers: for what fellowship hath righteousness with unrighteousness? and what communion hath light with darkness?*

Romans 12:2 *And be not conformed to this world: but be ye transformed by the renewing of your mind, that ye may prove what is that good, and acceptable, and perfect, will of God.*

Being involved with sinners can cause you to produce bad fruit. God sees how you act at home. He knows what is in your heart. Do not be a hypocrite. I try to be transparent with those around me when I mess up. I am honest about the things I have done in my life which I know are sinful. I do not try to act like I am perfect. I tell others about my mistakes, but I also tell them about my loving and forgiving savior.

Matthew 7:15 *Beware of false prophets, which come to you in sheep's clothing, but inwardly they are ravening wolves.*

Job 8:13-14 *So are the paths of all that forget God; and the hypocrite's hope shall perish: Whose hope shall be cut off, and whose trust shall be a spider's web.*

Genisis 6:13 *And God said unto Noah, The end of all flesh is come before me; for the earth is filled with violence through them; and, behold, I will destroy them with the earth.*

Deuteronomy 6:15 *(For the LORD thy God is a jealous God among you) lest the anger of the LORD thy God be kindled against thee, and destroy thee from off the face of the earth.*

Deuteronomy 7:23 *But the LORD thy God shall deliver them unto thee, and shall destroy them with a mighty destruction, until they be destroyed.*

Psalm 52:5 *God shall likewise destroy thee for ever, he shall take thee away, and pluck thee out of thy dwelling place, and root thee out of the land of the living. Selah.*

1 Corinthians 3:17 *If any man defile the temple of God, him shall God destroy; for the temple of God is holy, which temple ye are.*

What is God showing you in the garden?

_____

_____

_____

_____

_____

You will know them by their fruits.

Matthew 7:16-20 *Ye shall know them by their fruits. Do men gather grapes of thorns, or figs of thistles? Even so every good tree bringeth forth good fruit; but a corrupt tree bringeth forth evil fruit. A good tree cannot bring forth evil fruit, neither can a corrupt tree bring forth good fruit. Every tree that bringeth not forth good fruit is hewn down, and cast into the fire. Wherefore by their fruits ye shall know them.*

John 13:34-35 *A new commandment I give unto you, That ye love one another; as I have loved you, that ye also love one another. By this shall all men know that ye are my disciples, if ye have love one to another.*

John 15:7-14 *If ye abide in me, and my words abide in you, ye shall ask what ye will, and it shall be done unto you. Herein is my Father glorified, that ye bear much fruit; so shall ye be my disciples.*

John 15:9-14 *As the Father hath loved me, so have I loved you: continue ye in my love. If ye keep my commandments, ye shall abide in my love; even as I have kept my Father's commandments, and abide in his love. These things have I spoken unto you, that my joy might remain in you, and that your joy might be full. This is my commandment, That ye love one another, as I have loved you. Greater love hath no man than this, that a man lay down his life for his friends. Ye are my friends, if ye do whatsoever I command you.*

The fruit of **LOVE** is a powerful tool to win others to Christ. We are to love sinners, not the sin. The ultimate sacrifice of one's life for another is love. That is what Christ did for us. Jesus Christ gave His life for you and me.

We are not to judge and condemn others. It is our duty as a Christian to show everyone **LOVE.** Go out into the world and invite the lost into church. Witness to all those around us. When others do us wrong, we are to love them and pray for them. Being friendly and kind to those who are not just like us is one way to show love.

1 Corinthians 13:13 *And now abideth faith, hope, charity, these three; but the greatest of these is charity.*

Matthew 5:44 *But I say unto you, Love your enemies, bless them that curse you, do good to them that hate you, and pray for them which despitefully use you, and persecute you;*

Luk 6:27-28 *But I say unto you which hear, Love your enemies, do good to them which hate you, Bless them that curse you, and pray for them which despitefully use you.*

Luk 6:35 *But love ye your enemies, and do good, and lend, hoping for nothing again; and your reward shall be great, and ye shall be the children of the Highest: for he is kind unto the unthankful and to the evil.*

Think of when you did something wrong. Was there someone in your life that showed you love even when you were bad?

_____

_____

_____

_____

_____

The next fruit of the spirit is ***JOY.*** Joy is a happiness of the heart. Some people are just very cheerful and always have ways to make people around them smile. Joyful people are a pleasure to be around. Sometimes as a Christian, we have an inner joy that shines out as we go through life.

Psalm 32:11 *Be glad in the LORD, and rejoice, ye righteous: and shout for joy, all ye that are upright in heart.*

Proverb 15:23 *A man hath joy by the answer of his mouth: and a word spoken in due season, how good is it!*

Act 13:52 *And the disciples were filled with joy, and with the Holy Ghost.*

Romans 14:17 *For the kingdom of God is not meat and drink; but righteousness, and peace, and joy in the Holy Ghost.*

Romans 15:13 *Now the God of hope fill you with all joy and peace in believing, that ye may abound in hope, through the power of the Holy Ghost.*

Nehemiah 8:10 *Then he said unto them, Go your way, eat the fat, and drink the sweet, and send portions unto them for whom nothing is prepared: for this day is holy unto our Lord: neither be ye sorry; for the joy of the LORD is your strength.*

DO YOU HAVE THE JOY OF THE LORD IN YOU?

_____

_____

_____

_____

_____

PEACE is the next fruit of the spirit. Oh, the peace of God is so wonderful. When you accept Jesus Christ as your personal Savior, He fills you with a joy and a sweet peace. This is a tranquility of the mind, free from worry and fear. Even when trials come our way, we can still have peace in our hearts.

As a Christian we are to try to keep peace among us. We are not to stir up strife. God is a loving peaceful God. He does not like trouble. That does not mean we are to stand idly by and let sin go on. We are to take a stand for Christ and let people know when they are in sin. Jesus himself was a peaceful loving person, however He also took a stand.

When my oldest son was in eighth grade, we did a fund raiser by having the football moms play flag football. All was well and fun until our last practice the day before the game when I heard they had made baseball caps that said "*the other team*" *sucks.* I immediately went to the coach and told him if this were true and they were going to wear those, I would not participate. My son or I would not be at the game. I teach a Sunday school class, and this would not be sportsmanship behavior nor very Christian behavior.

To my surprise, this was true and at that moment, he said they would not wear them, and he would throw them away. Later another mother came up to me and apologized because she should have spoken up as well. Her and her husband did not like it either, but neither had taken a stand. Never be ashamed to take a stand for God. God will give you an internal peace as you make a bold step for Him.

James 3:18 *And the fruit of righteousness is sown in peace of them that make peace.*

Matthew 21:12 *And Jesus went into the temple of God, and cast out all them that sold and bought in the temple, and overthrew the tables of the moneychangers, and the seats of them that sold doves,*

Luke 24:36 *And as they thus spake, Jesus himself stood in the midst of them, and saith unto them, Peace be unto you.*

Proverbs 15:17-18 *Better is a dinner of herbs where love is, than a stalled ox and hatred therewith. A wrathful man stirreth up strife: but he that is slow to anger appeaseth strife.*

Romans 13:13 *Let us walk honestly, as in the day; not in rioting and drunkenness, not in chambering and wantonness, not in strife and envying.*

Romans 5:1 *Therefore being justified by faith, we have peace with God through our Lord Jesus Christ:*

Romans 14:17-19 *For the kingdom of God is not meat and drink; but righteousness, and peace, and joy in the Holy Ghost. For he that in these things serveth Christ is acceptable to God, and approved of men. Let us therefore follow after the things which make for peace, and things wherewith one may edify another.*

One of the fruits of the spirit is **LONG-SUFFERING.** One meaning is being patient with others. When others around us have problems or not doing things as we want it, we must be patient and let God do the work. Also quietly bearing injury is a meaning to this. We ourselves must learn not to complain all the time. We should have self-restraint. Do not be quick to anger.

Numbers 14:18 *The LORD is long suffering, and of great mercy, forgiving iniquity and transgression, and by no means clearing the guilty, visiting the iniquity of the fathers upon the children unto the third and fourth generation.*

Psalm 86:15 *But thou, O Lord, art a God full of compassion, and gracious, long suffering, and plenteous in mercy and truth.*

Colossians 3:12-13 *Put on therefore, as the elect of God, holy and beloved, bowels of mercies, kindness, humbleness of mind, meekness, longsuffering; Forbearing one another, and forgiving* *one another, if any man have a quarrel against any: even as Christ forgave you, so also do ye.*

Philippians 2:14 *Do all things without murmurings and disputings:*

The next fruit of the spirit is **GENTLENESS**. Gentleness is being kind and patient, not harsh or rough. We should be calm and gentle to those around us. I have been amazed at how God has shown me how the garden relates to our spiritual life with a calm gentle spirit. It is like a whisper to my soul.

2 Timothy 2:24 *And the servant of the Lord must not strive; but be gentle unto all men, apt to teach, patient,*

Titus 3:2 *To speak evil of no man, to be no brawlers, but gentle, shewing all meekness unto all men.*

James 3:17-18 *But the wisdom that is from above is first pure, then peaceable, gentle, and easy to be intreated, full of mercy and good fruits, without partiality, and without hypocrisy. And the fruit of righteousness is sown in peace of them that make peace.*

2 Corinthians 10:1 *Now I Paul myself beseech you by the meekness and gentleness of Christ, who in presence am base among you, but being absent am bold toward you:*

Then there is **GOODNESS.** This is a quality of being good. Also having virtue and being generous are aspects of goodness. We can show goodness by being generous with what God has given to us. We should desire to be a blessing to others.

2 Peter 1:3 *According as his divine power hath given unto us all things that pertain unto life and godliness, through the knowledge of him that hath called us to glory and virtue:*

2 Peter 1:5 *And beside this, giving all diligence, add to your faith virtue; and to virtue knowledge;*

2 Peter 1:5-9 *And beside this, giving all diligence, add to your faith virtue; and to virtue knowledge; And to knowledge temperance; and to temperance patience; and to patience godliness; And to godliness brotherly kindness; and to brotherly kindness charity. For if these things be in you, and abound, they make you that ye shall neither be barren nor unfruitful in the knowledge of our Lord Jesus Christ. But he that lacketh these things is blind, and cannot see afar off, and hath forgotten that he was purged from his old sins.*

FAITHFULNESS is the next fruit of the spirit. That is being loyal and dependable. We should always keep our word. Be honest in everything you do. Have faith in Jesus Christ. Others should be able to trust us and know we will do what we say we will do. Do not make promises you cannot keep. If I am not sure I can do something, I will say, I will try, but I cannot make promises.

We must believe in the Word of God. Have faith that He can do what He says He can do, and He will do what He says He will do. When we believe in the Word, we have faith. When others can depend on us to do what we say we will do, they have faith in us.

Rom 1:17 *For therein is the righteousness of God revealed from faith to faith: as it is written, The just shall live by faith.*

Rom 5:1-2 *Therefore being justified by faith, we have peace with God through our Lord Jesus Christ: By whom also we have access by faith into this grace wherein we stand, and rejoice in hope of the glory of God.*

Proverbs 14:5 *A faithful witness will not lie: but a false witness will utter lies.*

Proverbs 20:6-7 *Most men will proclaim every one his own goodness: but a faithful man who can find? The just man walketh in his integrity: his children are blessed after him.*

Luke 19:17 *And he said unto him, Well, thou good servant: because thou hast been faithful in a very little, have thou authority over ten cities.*

1 Corinthians 4:2 *Moreover it is required in stewards, that a man be found faithful.*

Read Hebrew chapter 11.

Our next fruit of the spirit is **MEEKNESS.** Meekness is gentleness, that is patient. It is being submissive. To be meek is to be exceedingly kind and gentle, treating it as if it were fragile. It is also having consideration for others. Being humble and submissive is a sign of meekness. We should show meekness by always being willing to learn.

Zephaniah 2:3 *Seek ye the LORD, all ye meek of the earth, which have wrought his judgment; seek righteousness, seek meekness: it may be ye shall be hid in the day of the LORD'S anger.*

Instead of complaining, be patient and wait on God.

Psalm 22:26 *The meek shall eat and be satisfied: they shall praise the LORD that seek him: your heart shall live for ever.*

Psalm 25:9 *The meek will he guide in judgment: and the meek will he teach his way.*

Psalm 37:11 *But the meek shall inherit the earth; and shall delight themselves in the abundance of peace.*

Matthew 5:5 *Blessed are the meek: for they shall inherit the earth.*

1 Peter 3:4-5 *But let it be the hidden man of the heart, in that which is not corruptible, even the ornament of a meek and quiet spirit, which is in the sight of God of great price. For after this manner in the old time the holy women also, who trusted in God, adorned themselves, being in subjection unto their own husbands:*

Galatians 6:1 *Brethren, if a man be overtaken in a fault, ye which are spiritual, restore such an one in the spirit of meekness; considering thyself, lest thou also be tempted.*

2 Corinthians 10:1 *Now I Paul myself beseech you by the meekness and gentleness of Christ, who in presence am base among you, but being absent am bold toward you:*

TEMPERANCE is a fruit of the spirit more of us need to pray for. To be temperance is to have self-control or self-restraint in conduct. We must be able to control our lust and desires. Self-control is a good way to describe temperance. We should control our tongue and be careful with the words we use. Think before you speak. Will this edify and glorify God?

The flesh has desires that is not always right in the eyes of God. We need to fill our heart with the Word of God. Learn to live in the spirit not in the flesh. When we live in the spirit as God would have us do, we have the ability to overcome anger and forgive quickly. We can show love toward others instead of angry tempers.

2 Peter 1:5-7 *And beside this, giving all diligence, add to your faith virtue; and to virtue knowledge; And to knowledge temperance; and to temperance patience; and to patience godliness; And to godliness brotherly kindness; and to brotherly kindness charity.*

1 John 2:15-17 *Love not the world, neither the things that are in the world. If any man love the world, the love of the Father is not in him. For all that is in the world, the lust of the flesh, and the lust of the eyes, and the pride of life, is not of the Father, but is of the world. And the world passeth away, and the lust thereof: but he that doeth the will of God abideth for ever.*

Galatians 5:25 *If we live in the Spirit, let us also walk in the Spirit.*

You will know them by their fruits.

Mat 7:16-20 *Ye shall know them by their fruits. Do men gather grapes of thorns, or figs of thistles? Even so every good tree bringeth forth good fruit; but a corrupt tree bringeth forth evil fruit. A good tree cannot bring forth evil fruit, neither can a corrupt tree bring forth good fruit. Every tree that bringeth not forth good fruit is hewn down, and cast into the fire. Wherefore by their fruits ye shall know them.*

Does your life show the fruits of the spirit? We have discussed each one individually. Ask yourself which of these you possess and which of these do you need improvement in. Pray to the Heavenly Father for spiritual guidance.

Take time now to meditate on the fruits of the spirit. What areas in your life do you need to change?

_____

_____

_____

_____

_____

The Harvest

In the harvest season, we reap what we sow. If you plant corn, you harvest corn, if you plant tomatoes, you harvest tomatoes. The same goes for life in general; if you sow seeds of happiness, you reap happiness. If you sow seeds of doubt, you reap doubt. If you sow seeds of strife and bitterness, you reap strife and bitterness. We need to be sowing seeds of love, joy, peace, kindness, faithfulness, gentleness and self-control.

During harvest time, we gather our crops to eat and share with others. We preserve the extra by canning or freezing. In most cases, our preserved food is eaten within a year or sometimes two years. Then it is time to grow a garden again. We go through the process all over to create a new crop and harvest again. Each year as you garden, you learn new things. You grow and mature in the skills from trial and error or from education.

The same goes for our spiritual life. We cannot just read the Bible one time, go to church one time and expect to live a Christian life. We must be fed God's word repeatedly. As we read, and listen to the Word of God, we continue to be fed spiritually. We need to be fed daily as we also feed others daily.

As we sow spiritual seeds, we help others to grow, who in return will produce more seeds and feed others. As the chain goes, we may never know who all has been saved or fed spiritually just because of a seed in which we planted. There are times we witness seeing others being mentored and taught and grow in the love of God. As the years go by, they feed others. Then those will feed even more as the years go by. It will be a glorious reward when we get to heaven and hear the stories of others and discover it all started from the simple word, we gave to someone who in turn shared with others.

Maybe we are not a preacher, teacher or evangelist but the seed we plant could be the seed that leads to the one where a great evangelist is born, and millions are saved. Never stop sowing seeds of the fruit in which God has put inside of you. Pray and ask God to bless those around you and show you who to witness to or open doors for you to sow a seed. There are many verses in the bible about harvest. Below are just a few to read.

Exodus 34:22 - *And thou shalt observe the feast of weeks, of the firstfruits of wheat harvest, and the feast of ingathering at the year's end.*

Galatians 6:9 - *And let us not be weary in well doing: for in due season we shall reap, if we faint not.*

Genesis 8:22 - *While the earth remaineth, seedtime and harvest, and cold and heat, and summer and winter, and day and night shall not cease.*

Joel 3:13 - *Put ye in the sickle, for the harvest is ripe: come, get you down; for the press is full, the fats overflow; for their wickedness is great.*

Isaiah 9:3 - *Thou hast multiplied the nation, and not increased the joy: they joy before thee according to the joy in harvest, and as men rejoice when they divide the spoil.*

What kind of seeds are you sowing?

_____

_____

_____

_____

_____

_____

_____

_____

_____

_____

Listening to God

I have been listening to God in the garden. He showed me how everything in the garden related to my life. When we listen and allow God to speak to our hearts, we can hear God in everything we do. One of my hobbies is gardening. It allowed me to spend prayerful moments listening to God as He showed me how to relate gardening aspects to our spiritual lives. What are your hobbies? Could you be hearing God speak to you? Are you listening?

Whatsoever you do, do it for the glory of God. Learn to be positive and ask how can this glorify my Lord? Everyone has different talents and gifts. Use your gift for God. Learn to love and appreciate other's gifts as well. Think about your own talents and how you can use them for God.

We must learn to listen to Christ in everything we do. Some people like fishing or hunting. Use that time to enjoy the nature of God, while listening to what He is telling you. Others may enjoy cooking. I'm sure God can speak through that too. God can use anything even mechanics can listen to God while working on cars. No matter what your profession or hobby, listen to God.

Continue to sow seeds in all you do.

Mark 4:14-32
The sower soweth the word. And these are they by the way side, where the word is sown; but when they have heard, Satan cometh

immediately, and taketh away the word that was sown in their hearts. And these are they likewise which are sown on stony ground; who, when they have heard the word, immediately receive it with gladness; And have no root in themselves, and so endure but for a time: afterward, when affliction or persecution ariseth for the word's sake, immediately they are offended. And these are they which are sown among thorns; such as hear the word, And the cares of this world, and the deceitfulness of riches, and the lusts of other things entering in, choke the word, and it becometh unfruitful. And these are they which are sown on good ground; such as hear the word, and receive it, and bring forth fruit, some thirtyfold, some sixty, and some an hundred. And he said, So is the kingdom of God, as if a man should cast seed into the ground; And should sleep, and rise night and day, and the seed should spring and grow up, he knoweth not how. For the earth bringeth forth fruit of herself; first the blade, then the ear, after that the full corn. But when the fruit is brought forth, immediately he putteth in the sickle, because the harvest is come. And he said, Whereunto shall we liken the kingdom of God? or with what comparison shall we compare it? It is like a grain of mustard seed, which, when it is sown in the earth, is less than all the seeds that be in the earth: But when it is sown, it groweth up, and becometh greater than all herbs, and shooteth out great branches; so that the fowls of the air may lodge under the shadow of it.

Listen to God in your garden.

We all have our own lives and different lifestyles. My personal hobby was gardening. In and through that God spoke to me. What is your hobby? What kind of job do you do? Try paying attention to things that God may be telling you. Nothing happens by coincidence. All things happen for a reason. All things work together for the good of those who love the Lord and are called according to His purpose. Romans 8:28

Author Biography.

My name is Sarah Lawrence. I grew up in the small town of Englewood Tennessee. I accepted Jesus Christ as my Lord and Savior at the age of nine. My parents were Paul and Mary Tudor. I lost my dad to cancer several years ago. Although I still miss him, God has given me grace in the fact my parents were indeed great Christian people, and I will see him again in heaven. They taught my three brothers, my sister, and I a lot of good morals. I married Steve Long at age 21. We have two children, David and Cody Long. Steve always lived by "principles." My husband Steve died from cancer at the early age of forty-nine. This left me a widow at age 39.

After a few years of trials, God has blessed me with another godly husband who supports me in all my dreams. I look forward to writing many more books to help disciple Christians.

Shortly after my first marriage, I felt God calling me to teach His word. I grew up in church, however I sure did not think I knew enough to teach. I was about twenty-five when the first opportunity came for me to teach. God opened the doors, and I walked through. I taught a vacation bible school class, which in turn led to teaching a Sunday school class for ages 8-12. That eventually led to teaching teenagers and then being the youth leader. Years later in another *church I was blessed with being youth leader and leading a ladies bible study class.*

Over the years I have been blessed to be able to have a garden almost every year. There were a few years where I lived in an apartment after my first husband passed away. Even there I managed to plant a couple of tomato and cucumber plants up close to the bushes. I had just enough tomatoes and cucumbers for myself and sometimes enough to share with a neighbor. I simply can't seem to get enough gardening. It is my hobby or passion which gives me great joy.

I graduated with a Bachelor of Science degree, majoring in business management at the age of fifty. I have remarried and now have four grandchildren. Stay tuned for my next book, Listening to God Through Aprons. I love wearing an apron with my grandchildren while cooking and baking. This book will contain some of my favorite recipes along with real pictures with my grandchildren helping.

I may be contacted by email. *sanddlawrence@gmail.com*